Snails
Up Close

Greg Pyers

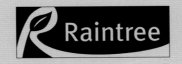

www.raintreepublishers.co.uk
Visit our website to find out more information about **Raintree** books.

To order:
☎ Phone 44 (0) 1865 888112
🗎 Send a fax to 44 (0) 1865 314091
💻 Visit the Raintree Bookshop at **www.raintreepublishers.co.uk** to browse our catalogue and order online.

First published 2005 by Heinemann Library
a division of Harcourt Education Australia,
18–22 Salmon Street, Port Melbourne Victoria 3207 Australia
(a division of Reed International Books Australia Pty Ltd,
ABN 70 001 002 357).
Visit the Heinemann Library website at
www.heinemannlibrary.com.au

Published in Great Britain by Raintree,
Halley Court, Jordan Hill, Oxford OX2 8EJ,
part of Harcourt Education
Raintree is a registered trademark of Harcourt Education Ltd.

℞ A Reed Elsevier company

© Reed International Books Australia Pty Ltd 2005

09 08 07 06 05
10 9 8 7 6 5 4 3 2 1

Editorial: Anne McKenna, Carmel Heron
Design: Kerri Wilson, Stella Vassiliou
Photo research: Legend Images, Wendy Duncan
Production: Tracey Jarrett
Illustration: Rob Mancini

Typeset in Officina Sans 19/23 pt
Film separations by Digital Imaging Group (DIG), Melbourne
Printed and bound in Hong Kong and China by South China
Printing Company Ltd.

The paper used to print this book comes from sustainable
resources.

National Library of Australia Cataloguing-in-Publication data:

Pyers, Greg.
  Snails up close.

  Includes index.
  For primary school students.
  ISBN 1 74070 233 6.

  1. Snails – Juvenile literature. I. Title.
  (Series: Minibeasts up close).

Acknowledgements
The publisher would like to thank the following for permission
to reproduce photographs: Auscape/Dinodia-OSF/I. Kehimkar:
p. **5**, /Tui De Roy: p. **11**, /Jean-Paul Ferrero: pp. **6**, **20**,
/Ferrero-Labat: p. **8**, /C. Andrew Henley: pp. **7**, **21**, **22**, **23**,
/OSF/Karen Gowlett-Holmes: p. **25**; Australian Picture Library
/Corbis: p. **29**; Getty Images/Taxi/Jeri Gleiter: p.**10**; © Dwight
Kuhn: pp. **12**, **15**; Lochman Transparencies/Clay Bryce: p. **4**,
/Len Stewart: p. **16**; photolibrary.com: pp. **14**, **17**, **24**, **28**,
/SPL: p. **13**; R. Goellner, Saint Louis Zoo: p. **27**; Shedd
Aquarium: p. **26**.

Cover photograph of a land snail reproduced with the
permission of Lochman Transparencies/Clay Bryce.

Every attempt has been made to trace and acknowledge
copyright. Where an attempt has been unsuccessful, the
publisher would be pleased to hear from the copyright owner
so any omission or error can be rectified.

594.3

Contents

Words that are printed in bold, **like this**, are explained in the glossary on page 31.

Amazing snails!

Most of us have seen snails at night. They glide slowly over footpaths, and up plant stems. Have you ever seen a snail during the day? Was it tucked up inside its shell? When you look at them up close, snails really are amazing animals.

If you look closely, you are sure to find a snail in a garden.

What are snails?

Snails are molluscs. A mollusc has a soft body without bones. Slugs, octopuses and limpets are also molluscs. Many molluscs, such as snails, have a hard shell.

There are many kinds of snails. In this book, we will look closely at the garden snail. This is the one you see most often. But we will also look at some other kinds of snails.

The largest snail is the giant African land snail. It grows to a length of 20 centimetres. The smallest snails are just 1.5 millimetres long.

Where do snails live?

A garden is one of the best places to find snails.

Vegetable gardens

A **habitat** is the place where an animal lives. A vegetable garden is a very good habitat for snails. There are many plants to eat and many places to hide from **predators**. There is also shade to protect the snails from the sun.

Snails eat the same kinds of plants that people eat. The leaves in a vegetable garden are soft and easy to chew.

6

Other snail habitats

There are about 20,000 kinds, or **species**, of snails. Most species live in water. Ponds are home to many kinds of freshwater snails. Some live in the mud at the bottom of ponds. Other species cling to pond weeds. Many kinds of snails live in the sea. Some of these snails are called periwinkles or whelks.

Periwinkles are often found in sheltered rock pools.

Snail body parts

A snail's body has three main parts. These are the head, the shell and the foot.

The head

The head of a garden snail has four **tentacles**, or feelers. There are two long tentacles and two short tentacles. There are eyes on the ends of the long tentacles. When the tentacles are touched, they shrink back into the snail's head. The snail's mouth is underneath the head.

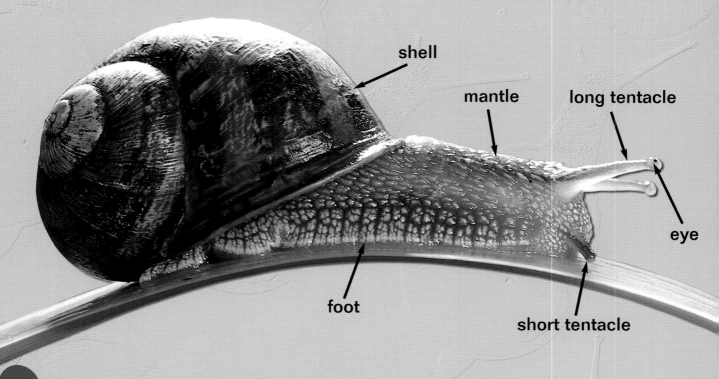

shell

mantle

long tentacle

eye

foot

short tentacle

The shell

The shell grows on a part of a snail's body called the **mantle**. The shell is attached to the snail's body by a muscle.

The foot

The long, lower part of a snail is called the foot. The bottom of the foot is called the sole. The sole touches the surface the snail is moving over. The skin of the foot is often bumpy. Parts of the foot produce a sticky **liquid** called **mucus**.

Slugs

Slugs are really snails without shells. In fact, some slugs have tiny shells on their backs.

A snail's shell

A snail's shell is shaped like a **spiral**. The spiral shape allows it to grow as the snail's body grows. The curves of the spiral are called whorls. As the shell grows, the whorls become wider. The shell stops growing when the snail becomes an adult. But the opening of the shell may develop a wider lip, which makes it stronger.

Protection

In dry weather, or when resting, a snail pulls itself into its shell. It plugs the shell up with **mucus**. The mucus dries and the snail stays moist inside.

A snail's shell keeps the animal from drying out.

Different shells

Different **species** of snails have different shells. The Haitian tree snail has a white shell with black, orange and red stripes. The garden snail has a brown shell. If you look at garden snails, you will see that each one has a slightly different shell.

Growth lines

A snail's shell has lines running across it. These lines mark the times when the shell was growing. The shell grows only when the snail is feeding.

This land snail from Komodo Island, Indonesia, has a beautiful yellow and red shell.

Mouthparts and eating

As any gardener knows, snails eat many kinds of plants. Snails really like leafy vegetables and flowers.

The mouth

A snail's mouth is underneath its head. It has two small lips. Just inside the upper lip is a hard part called a jaw. Just inside the lower lip is the snail's tongue. This is called a **radula**. The radula is covered in rows of tiny teeth.

This is the head of a garden snail. The mouth is underneath.

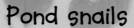

Pond snails

Pond snails use their radulas to feed on **algae**. Algae are tiny plants that grow in a pond.

This close-up photo shows the teeth on a snail's radula.

Feeding

When the snail is feeding, the jaw scrapes and cuts the food. The radula rubs against the jaw and the tiny teeth scrape and shred the food. The constant rubbing on food wears down the radula's teeth. Many teeth break off. The radula keeps growing so the snail always has new teeth.

Swallowing

The radula moves the tiny pieces of food further into the mouth to be swallowed.

Sight, smell and touch

Snails use their **senses** to find food, mates and safe places to shelter.

Eyes

A snail's eyes are at the tips of its long **tentacles**. But a snail cannot see things around it. All it can really see is dark and light. For a snail, this is very helpful. It can stay in shady places, which are moist. It can also keep out of sunny places, where it could dry out. There are other parts of a snail's **mantle**, foot and lips that also sense light.

eye

A garden snail's eyes look like black dots at the end of its long tentacles.

Smell

A snail's long tentacles also sense
smells. The snail waves its tentacles
about to pick up smells as they float through the air.

Up and down

Snails can sense which
way is up. Turn one over
and watch it right itself!

Touch

A snail's sense of touch is strongest around its head.
As a snail moves, its short tentacles feel the way
ahead. A snail pulls its tentacles into its body as
soon as they are touched. It may even go inside its
shell and let out bubbles of **mucus** to protect itself
from attack.

When danger is about,
a snail pulls itself into its shell.

Moving

Have you seen silvery trails winding across a concrete footpath? These trails show where snails have been the night before.

The foot

A snail glides along the ground on its large foot. The foot has rows of muscles that tighten and then relax and then tighten again. This causes ripples to flow from the head end to the tail end of the foot. These ripples make the snail move forward. You can see the ripples if you place a snail on a piece of glass and look underneath.

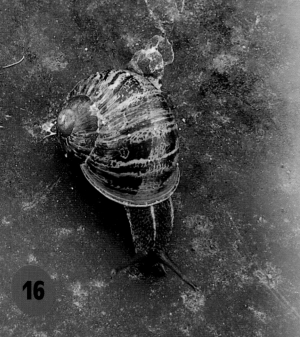

Silver trails of snails disappear when the sun dries them.

Mucus

The snail produces **mucus** to protect its foot from damage as it moves over rough surfaces. Mucus is a sticky, slimy **liquid** produced just below the snail's head. It leaves behind silver trails.

Staying moist

Mucus also comes from the snail's **mantle**. It spreads over the snail's body and helps to protect it against drying out.

Because mucus is sticky, a snail is able to move over slippery surfaces.

Inside a snail

Inside a snail, all the parts seem to be in the strangest places!

How do snails get air?

Garden snails breathe air through a hole near the edge of their shell. The air travels to the snail's **lung**. The lung takes the part of the air called **oxygen** into the blood.

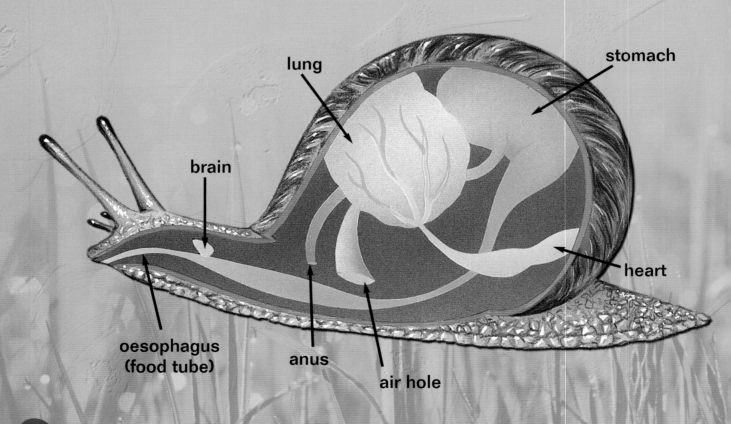

lung

stomach

brain

heart

oesophagus
(food tube)

anus

air hole

Blood

A snail's blood is a kind of blue colour. It is pumped by the heart through tubes called **arteries**. When the blood leaves the arteries, it moves through the spaces in the snail's body. The blood makes its way back to the heart to be pumped around again.

What happens to food?

After food is swallowed, it moves along a food tube to the stomach. The food is broken down to release **nutrients**. A snail needs nutrients to survive. Waste passes out through the anus.

The brain

A snail's brain gets information from the **senses**, mostly through its eyes and **tentacles**. It sends messages to the rest of the body about what to do.

Snail eggs

One of the most amazing things about garden snails is that each snail is both a male and a female.

Mating time

When two snails **mate**, they swap **sperm**. Sperm are produced by the male part of each snail. The sperm join with the eggs that each snail has inside its body. After this happens, a tiny snail will start to form within each egg.

These two garden snails are mating.

Laying eggs

A snail lays its eggs about two weeks after mating. First it digs a small hole in moist soil. Then the snail pushes its eggs out through an opening behind its head. The snail may lay more eggs later in another hole. There may be up to 50 eggs laid in each hole. The snail leaves its eggs. In warm weather the eggs will hatch in about two weeks.

Underwater snail

The giant pond snail lays its eggs in a sticky group attached to plants, rocks or other underwater objects.

These garden snail eggs are safely hidden in damp soil.

Growing up

When a young snail hatches from its egg, it has a see-through body. Its shell is soft and pale.

First meal

The first thing a snail does after hatching is to eat its eggshell. It then looks for tiny pieces of plant to eat. In a few days, it leaves its hole. It grows quickly. In two weeks its shell becomes hard and brown. The snail's body becomes darker.

newly hatched snail

This garden snail has just hatched. It will now eat its eggshell.

Half grown

After six months, the snail is half grown. Its shell has three whorls, or curves. Three months later the snail is almost fully grown and its shell has four whorls.

Snail lifespan

Most garden snails live for three or four years. Some might reach eight years of age. In its lifetime, a snail will probably lay at least 500 eggs.

Adult snail

One year after hatching, the snail has become an adult. Its shell will not grow any larger, but it will become thicker and stronger. When it is two years old, it will find a mate. Soon afterwards, it will lay eggs of its own.

This garden snail is about six months old.

Aquatic snails

Aquatic snails live in water. These snails have many things in common with land snails. They have many differences too.

Breathing

Like fish, some aquatic snails have **gills**. Gills allow these snails to get **oxygen** under water. Other aquatic snails, such as the giant pond snail, have a **lung**. A lung takes oxygen from the air. Aquatic snails with a lung have a tube, called a **siphon**, which they put above the water's surface to reach the air.

This giant pond snail breathes through a lung.

Shell

Most aquatic snails have a **spiral** shell. Some **species** have thick shells that few **predators** can bite through. Sea snails, such as whelks, live on the seashore. They have a door in their shells and they can close this tightly when the tide is out. This keeps them from drying out.

A whelk has a thick shell with a little door in it.

Producing young

While each land snail has both male and female parts, many aquatic snails are either male or female. There are even some female pond snails that can lay eggs without having to **mate**.

Endangered snails

The partula snails of the island of Moorea in the Pacific Ocean are among the most **endangered** animals on Earth. This story of three snails explains why.

Giant African snails

In the 1960s, giant African snails began to invade the forests of Moorea. These snails had been kept to sell to restaurants in other countries. But many escaped and became serious pests on the farms of Moorea.

Partula snails live in forests and banana plantations on the Pacific island of Moorea.

Rosy wolf snails

To control the giant African snails, the farmers of Moorea brought the rosy wolf snail to their island. This snail is **carnivorous**, which means it eats meat. The farmers hoped that it would eat the giant African snails. But it did not.

Partula snails

Partula snails are unusual because they can lay eggs, or give birth to live snails. But about ten years after the carnivorous snails were brought to Moorea, partula snails had almost disappeared. The rosy wolf snails had eaten most of them.

This zoo produces partula snails.

Snails and us

To gardeners, snails can be pests because they eat vegetables and plants. Other people only ever notice the snails that crack and squash underfoot on a dark, wet night. But these are not the only ways people and snails affect each other.

You can learn a lot about snails just by watching them.

Pest snails

The green snail from southern Europe has appeared in Western Australia. It arrived there with an airline passenger who thought they might be good to eat. Instead, it became a pest. If not controlled, this snail could seriously damage Western Australia's vegetable-growing industry.

Pet snails

Many people who have aquariums keep pond snails, such as apple snails. These snails have colourful shells. They clean up the **algae** that grow in the aquarium, and help to keep it clean.

This apple snail lives in a home aquarium.

Find out for yourself

You are sure to find snails in a garden. During the day, look in dark, damp places under bushes. At night, snails are easy to find because they come out to feed.

Books to read

Looking at Minibeasts: Slugs and Snails, Sally Morgan (Belitha Press, 2001)

Heinemann First Library – Bug Books: Snail, Karen Hartley and Chris Macro (Heinemann Library, 1998)

Using the Internet

Explore the Internet to find out more about snails. Websites can change, so do not worry if the links below no longer work. Use a search engine, such as www.yahooligans.com or www.internet4kids.com, and type in a keyword such as 'pond snail' or 'garden snail'.

Websites

http://www.geocities.com/Athens/Atrium/5924/snaillinks.htm
This site has a variety of information about snails, including how to keep snails as pets.

http://members.tripod.com/arnobrosi/snail.html
This site has many interesting facts about snail **species**, including information about snails in literature and art.

Glossary

algae   tiny water plants

aquatic   living in water

arteries   tubes that carry blood

carnivorous   meat-eating

endangered   at risk of becoming extinct

gill   part of an aquatic snail's body that helps it breathe underwater

habitat   place where an animal lives

liquid   something that is runny, not hard, such as juice

lung   part of the body that fills with air as an animal breathes

mantle   soft part of a snail's body

mate   when a male and a female come together to produce young

mucus   sticky liquid

nutrients   parts of food that are important for an animal's health

oxygen   gas in the air that is needed for life

predator   animal that kills and eats other animals

radula   snail's tongue

sense   how an animal knows what is going on around it, such as seeing, hearing or smelling

siphon   tube through which some snails breathe

species   type or kind of animal

sperm   tiny cell produced by the male part of a snail

spiral   curve that begins small and becomes larger

tentacle   feeler on a snail's head

Index